KNOWLEDGE ENCYCLOPEDIA
RENAISSANCE ART

© Wonder House Books 2021

All rights reserved. No part of this book may be reproduced or transmitted in any form by any means, electronic or mechanical, including photocopying and recording, or by any information storage and retrieval system except as may be expressly permitted in writing by the publisher.

(An imprint of Prakash Books)

contact@wonderhousebooks.com

Disclaimer: The information contained in this encyclopedia has been collated with inputs from subject experts. All information contained herein is true to the best of the Publisher's knowledge.

Maps are only indicative in nature.

ISBN : 9789390391561

Table of Contents

Renaissance Art	3
Renaissance in the Low Countries	4–5
German Renaissance	6–7
Quattrocento	8–9
Early Renaissance Paintings	10–11
The Medici Influence	12–13
Italian High Renaissance	14–15
Leonardo da Vinci (1452–1519)	16–17
Michelangelo (1475–1564)	18–19
The Sistine Chapel	20–21
Raphael (1483–1520)	22–23
The School of Athens	24–25
Renaissance in Venice	26–27
Mannerism	28–29
El Greco (1541–1614)	30–31
Word Check	32

RENAISSANCE **ART**

The period between 1400–1600 saw a revival of Greek and Roman art styles in Europe. This period is therefore called **Renaissance**, the French word for 'rebirth'. Artists adopted oil paintings and created sculptures in marble and bronze. Attention to light, detail and colour were hallmarks of the Renaissance in northern Europe.

Some of the greatest contributions to Renaissance art came from the Italian states of Florence, Rome and Venice. It was driven by the ideas of **humanism**, which reject religious stereotypes and focus on the individual. Artists studied human bodies to understand movement and expression. Many new techniques were developed to express reality in art.

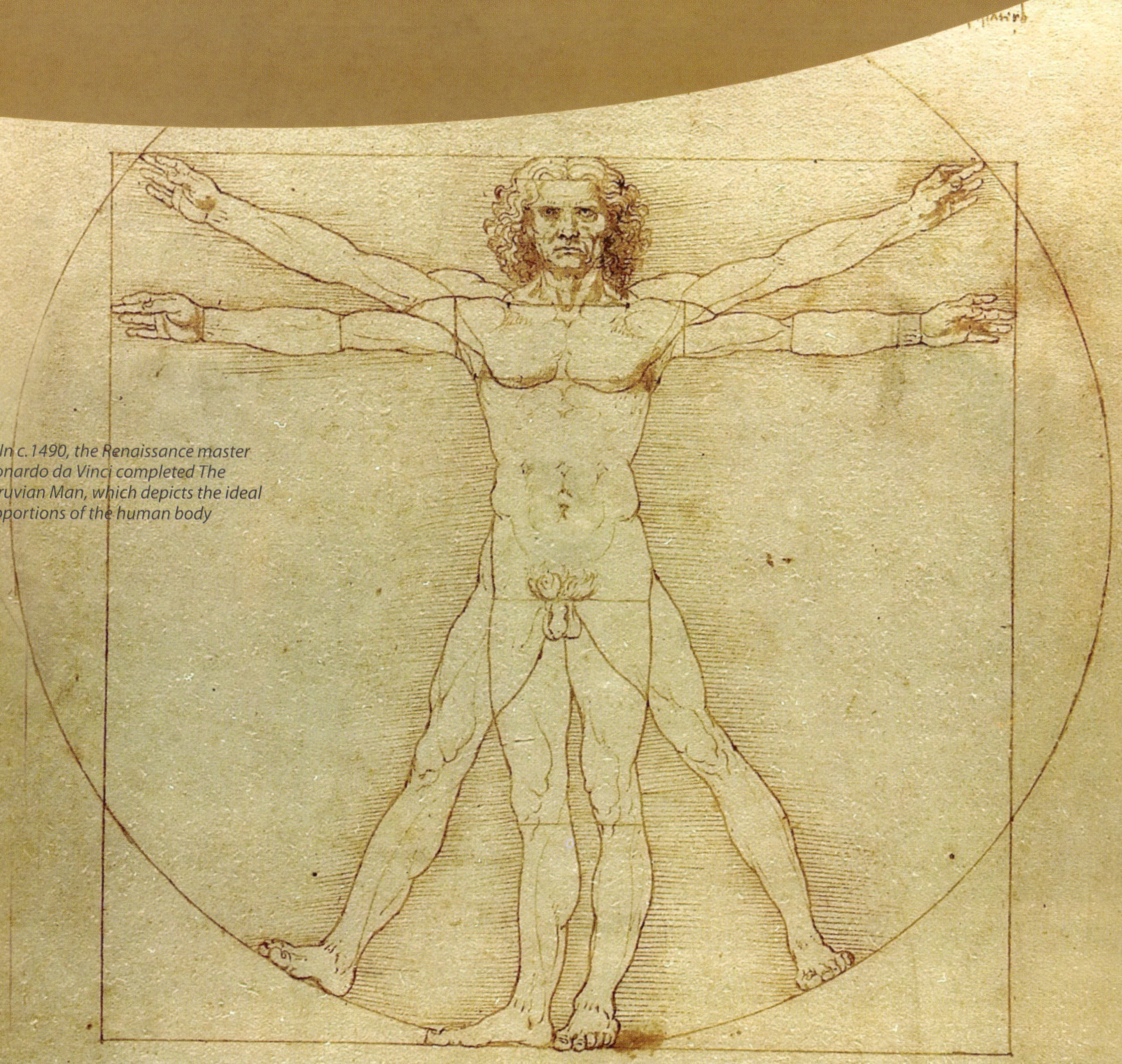

▶ *In c. 1490, the Renaissance master Leonardo da Vinci completed The Vitruvian Man, which depicts the ideal proportions of the human body*

Renaissance in the Low Countries

'Low Countries' is the historic name for the area covering the present-day countries of Belgium, Luxembourg and the Netherlands. The people who lived here were Dutch and Flemish. Their Renaissance extended over the 15th and 16th centuries. In the early years, most artworks were made for the Church. Around 1530, the region split along religious lines, into Flemish Catholics and Dutch Protestants. This divide is also reflected in the art from the Renaissance period.

Van Eyck Brothers

The Flemish brothers Hubert van Eyck (c.1366–1426) and Jan van Eyck (c.1390–1441) were the founders and masters of the Netherlandish Renaissance. Working with oil paints, they reached a level of brilliance never seen before. The Ghent Altarpiece at St Bavo's Cathedral is their masterpiece. The side panels of this **polyptych** could be folded over the central panels. It shows Christ the King, Virgin Mary and John the Baptist looking upon a gathering of saints, sinners, priests and soldiers. They attend the adoration of Jesus, who appears as the Lamb of God. At the very end are Adam and Eve.

▲ *The open view of the Ghent Altarpiece, done with oil paints on wooden panels, c.1432*

▲ *The closed view of the Ghent Altarpiece shows prophets, patrons and angels*

The Arnolfini Portrait

Jan van Eyck left behind many works. One of his most famous works is the *Arnolfini Portrait* (1434), which shows a wealthy businessman and his expectant wife. In an era when most art was religious and public, this unusual piece was secular and private.

Van Eyck used layer after layer of paint to give a bright, mirror-like effect to the whole picture. Oil paint allowed him to create fine details. Notice the vivid textures of wood, velvet, metal, etc., the careful folds of the clothes and the many variations of light. The portrait looks as real as life—a breakthrough effect of the Renaissance.

▶ *The portrait was supposedly of Giovanni Arnolfini and his wife*

RENAISSANCE ART

Robert Campin and Rogier van der Weyden

The van Eyck brothers painted for the nobility. On the other hand, Robert Campin (c.1378–1444) painted for middle-class patrons. He is also called the Master of Flémalle for his Flemish style of painting. His most famous pupil is Rogier van der Weyden. The works of both artists show deep emotion and religious passion. Van der Weyden is particularly known for creating interesting spaces and slender figures.

▲ Campin's Merode Altarpiece was a triptych (3-panel art) of the Annunciation, showing how the stiff and flat styles of Gothic art were turning into the more realistic forms of Renaissance art

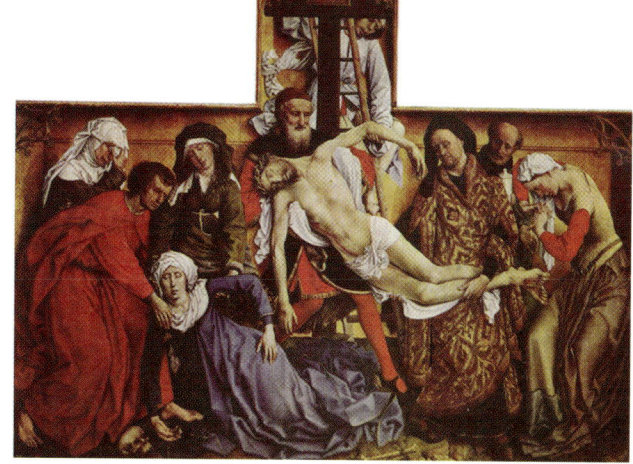

▲ Van der Weyden's Descent from the Cross, painted in primary colours, shows incredibly realistic emotion and movement

Hieronymus Bosch

In the 15th century, the Netherlands was full of religious fanatics. Their extreme behaviour inspired Bosch's paintings. He painted Heaven, Hell and Earth, using fabulous landscapes and dream-like images. Bosch's **surreal** art is filled with **symbolism**.

◀ The Garden of Earthly Delights shows the Garden of Eden and Hell on the left and right respectively. In between lies a busy world of human activity. Each group of figures tells its own story

Pieter Bruegel the Elder

Flemish master Pieter Bruegel the Elder (c.1525–1569) painted amazing and large compositions. Mountains, rivers, cities, and ships were a part of his landscapes. Each work had a moral lesson. His *Tower of Babel* is a warning against arrogance. The works also show great attention to detail and a sensitive use of light and shade.

◀ The Tower of Babel, 1563

German Renaissance

Renaissance took off in the modern regions of Germany and Austria around 1450. It was aided by the invention of the printing press by the German inventor, Johannes Gutenberg. There were also other innovations, such as oil-based ink and many types of moulds and matrices, that spread the ideas of Renaissance. As a result, printmaking, woodcuts, etchings and engravings dominated the German Renaissance. Religious panel paintings and wood carvings were also popular.

▲ *The carved and painted centrepiece of the St Wolfgang Altarpiece is a masterwork of sculptor-painter Michael Pacher, one of the earliest artists to introduce Renaissance principles to Germany*

▲ *Court painter Lucas Cranach the Elder (1472–1553) drew many portraits, including one of his friend Martin Luther, the man who brought about Protestantism, a new form of Christianity*

▲ *The printmaker Martin Schongauer is famous for his Madonna of the Rose Garden (1473)*

Albrecht Dürer (1471–1528)

Albrecht Dürer is possibly the greatest figure of the German Renaissance. He was the son of a goldsmith. Inspired by the High Renaissance of Italy, Dürer learned mathematics and geometry to perfect his art. These helped him create harmony and realism in his compositions. Dürer also studied **anatomy** and human nature. As a result, his line drawings seemed to have a life of their own. Dürer's talent also lay in using magnificent colours and a particular way of painting light.

▲ *Dürer's skill as a draughtsman can be seen in a 1508 piece called Praying Hands*

◀ *One of Dürer's most famous paintings depicts the martyrdom of 10,000 Christian soldiers on Mount Ararat, carried out by Shahpur I, the King of Persia, under orders from the Roman Emperor*

In Real Life

A pioneer of modern book illustrations, Dürer drew artworks for his own books. These include his *Four Books on Human Proportions* and *Four Books on Measurement* (1525). These are still available to artists today.

▲ *Albrecht Dürer's self-portrait at the age of 28*

Matthias Grünewald (c.1470–1528)

Little is known about Matthias Grünewald, a skilled Renaissance creator of Christian art in Germany. His colouring techniques were centuries ahead of his time. Because of this, only a few contemporaries understood his genius. His greatest work perhaps was displayed in the hospital of the Monastery of St Anthony in Isenheim. It is called the Isenheim Altarpiece and is a polyptych. When closed, it shows the crucifixion of Christ. Christ's agony is shown in his painfully thin and marred body with horrific large nails driven through his hands and feet. This realistic and symbolic torment of the saviour is meant to reflect a pain the patients and their families were all too familiar with; but there is also the hope of salvation.

◀ The Isenheim Altarpiece created between 1512 and 1516

Hans Holbein the Younger (1497–1543)

While Gothic art is focused on the divine, Renaissance is all about the human condition. Influenced by Humanism, the brilliant Hans Holbein became the greatest portrait painter of Europe during his lifetime. Before he had turned 20, he was already famous for his portraits of *Erasmus of Rotterdam* (1523), the *Darmstadt Madonna* (1526), the *Astronomer Nicholas Kratzer* (1528) and *Sir Thomas More* (1527).

In 1532, Holbein became the artist of the English court. With skill and precision, he made magnificent portraits of King Henry VIII, Thomas Cromwell and many others. He also created festive paintings and designs for jewellery and precious objects.

▲ Holbein's painting of the English lawyer and statesman, Sir Thomas More, who was executed by Henry VIII for upholding his religious beliefs

The Cologne School of Art

During the Renaissance, Cologne was a wealthy and secure city. Most important among the painters from the Cologne School of Art was the precise, detailed artist Stefan Lochner (c.1410–1451). He created a soft style of oil painting noted for its amazing hues and delicate emotions.

◀ Lochner's altarpieces used flowing lines and gem-like colours, as seen in this painting called the Last Judgement (c.1435)

Isn't It Amazing!

Holbein produced over 1,200 drawings from woodcuts! The best-known series amongst these is called the *Dance of Death*. It shows a skeletal death mocking humanity, from emperors and judges to merchants and farmers.

Quattrocento

In Italy, the artistic period of the 15th century is called the Quattrocento. Italy was not a unified country but a group of independent city-states. Among them were Florence, Rome and Venice. The Renaissance flourished foremost in these three cities.

▶ *Art of the Quattrocento moved away from divine perfection to the study of the individual. This is captured in the sinuous bodies and brutal emotions of Hercules and Antaeus, a bronze statue by Antonio del Pollaiuolo*

 ## From the Beginning

The Quattrocento began in Florence with a competition over who would design the eastern doors of the **Baptistery** of San Giovanni. It was won by the goldsmith and painter Lorenzo Ghiberti. Filippo Brunelleschi and Donatello, who were defeated in the competition, left for Rome. There, they studied the sculpture and architecture of ancient Rome. When they returned to Florence, they put their Classical knowledge to practical use. Thus began the Renaissance.

◀ *The major Italian city-states of the late 15th century*

◀ *The story of Joseph, a panel from the second set of doors to the Baptistery designed by Ghiberti*

 ## A Matter of Perspective

Have you ever noticed that faraway objects look smaller than the objects that are close by? A tree outside your window will look smaller than the pencil in your hand. This is because our brains do not see things as they are. They see objects relative to the position of other objects. This manner of seeing things is called perspective.

Naturally, your perspective changes when you move. Drawing sizes, angles and shapes of objects according to perspective needs a lot of practice and skill. It also needs an understanding of math and geometry. Such mathematical knowledge was brought back into art by Renaissance sculptor and designer Filippo Brunelleschi. It spread across Europe and other artists added their own knowledge to it. It is seen as a hallmark of Renaissance art.

▶ *Andrea Mantegna (1431–1506) painted St Sebastian to look like a sculpture. He also played with perspective by lowering the horizon. This gives the whole piece a monumental appearance*

Donatello (1386–1466)

Donato di Niccolò di Betto Bardi is better known simply as Donatello. He is often thought to be the finest sculptor of the Quattrocento. He put such movement and emotion into his statues that they seemed to come alive. Donatello's masterpiece is a 5-foot-tall, bronze sculpture of David. The young Biblical shepherd is seen as a slender, confident boy wearing a hat and boots. He stands over the head of his enemy Goliath, who he has slain, holding Goliath's long sword.

▶ An early bronze relief sculpture of Donatello, The Feast of Herod

Andrea del Verrocchio (c.1435–1488)

Inspired by Donatello, Verrocchio created sculptures that were just as amazing. In particular, his statue of the **condottiere** Bartolomeo Colleoni (1480s) shows bold, swaggering movement. His bronze figure of a *putto* (a small boy, a cherub or cupid) with a dolphin was a breakthrough in freestanding Renaissance sculpture. The boy is balanced on one leg and looks like he could topple over, but he does not. In fact, the overall design gives every angle of this figure equal importance.

Lady with Primroses

Created over 1475–1480, the *Lady with Primroses* created a new type of Renaissance **bust**. As with ancient Roman statues, the arms were also shown here. This allowed the artist to express emotion through the face as well as body language.

▶ Verrocchio's Lady with Primroses shows a woman dreamily holding flowers to her bosom

◀ Putto with Dolphin, c.1470

Incredible Individuals

Verrocchio was a talented painter. He owned a large studio-cum-workshop that attracted many, many students. Among them was none other than the foremost of Renaissance masters Leonardo da Vinci.

▶ Experts believe that some parts of Verrocchio's painting Tobias and the Angel were done by Leonardo da Vinci

Early Renaissance Paintings

The Italian Renaissance crept in during the 14th century, a time period called the Trecento. An early master painter of the period was Giotto di Bondone (c.1267–1337). He moved away from the flat and idealised drawings of the Gothic era. Instead, he made simple, clear paintings that were true to nature and showed the depths of humanity. For almost 700 years, he was worshipped as the Father of European painting. Tragically, 14th-century Italy was devastated by terrible wars and the Great Plague. It was only in the Quattrocento that Renaissance painting truly took hold in Italy.

▲ The Entry into Jerusalem by Giotto shows the gradual change from flat Gothic paintings to the emotional, individualistic figures of Renaissance

▲ The Queen of Sheba Meets King Solomon is part of The Legend of the True Cross, a series of early Renaissance frescoes by Piero della Francesca, an artist and mathematician

Masaccio (1401–1428)

The founder and the first master of Quattrocento paintings is nicknamed Masaccio. The first 21 years of his life are not documented. Then, in just six years, he entirely changed the style of Florentine painting. Though he lived a short life, his work laid the foundations for Western art. Masaccio's work showed scholarly thinking. It was composed on a grand scale. He introduced a never-before-seen degree of Naturalism into each painting.

◀ Masaccio's Holy Trinity is painted in such a way, it appears to be three-dimensional. This technique is called the tromp l'oeil, meaning deceiving the eye

The Brancacci Chapel

Over 1425–1427, Masaccio painted a series of frescoes inspired by the life of St Peter. Located in the Brancacci Chapel, these masterpieces are large and dramatic. The painting of Adam and Eve, as they are expelled from the Garden of Eden, shows the couple writhing in distress. Eve's expression especially shows a feeling of great despair. After Masaccio's death, the Renaissance talent Filippino Lippi completed the fresco cycle.

▶ Masaccio's Expulsion of Adam and Eve, 1427

RENAISSANCE ART

▲ St Peter heals a disabled person and raises Tabitha from the dead, a Brancacci fresco by Masaccio

🏛 Fra Angelico (1400–1455)

Guido di Pietro, also called Fra Angelico, is one of the greatest 15th-century painters. His early Renaissance work reflects a calm and religious style. Strongly influenced by Classical Rome, Fra Angelico carefully composed his paintings according to the rules of perspective.

💡 Isn't It Amazing!

The Brancacci Chapel rapidly became a training place for young artists. They came to copy the frescoes and refine their own skills. Among them was a young Michelangelo, whose Sistine Chapel frescoes were influenced by Masaccio's art.

▶ Michelangelo's The Fall and Expulsion from the Garden of Eden, painted on the ceiling of the Sistine Chapel in 1509, shows Masaccio's influence

◀ Commissioned by the Pope, Angelico's St Lawrence Distributing Alms (1447) uses lavish designs, expensive colours, gilded figures and gold leaf motifs

🏛 Fra Filippo Lippi (1406–1469)

Though deeply influenced by Masaccio and Angelico, Fra Filippo Lippi had his own style of painting. His *Coronation of the Virgin* is a historic and complex piece. It is the first example of a single vast scene spread over multiple panels. The painter Fra Diamante was Lippi's companion and colleague. Together, they decorated parts of the cathedral of Prato, a lively city near Florence. His work at the cathedral is some of Lippi's best art.

▶ Adoration in the Forest by Fra Filippo Lippi, 1459

🏛 Sandro Botticelli (1445–1510)

Fra Lippi's most famous student, Botticelli, created paintings filled with the spirit of Renaissance. His world-famous *Birth of Venus* and *Primavera* showcase his love for pale colours and graceful figures. Botticelli painted fanciful, yet deeply symbolic scenes from mythology.

▲ Primavera (Spring) by Botticelli shows mythological figures in a garden

◀ The Birth of Venus shows the Roman Goddess of love risen from the sea. To her left are the wind god Zephyr and the nymph Chloris or Aura. To her right is an attendant goddess bearing a cloak

The Medici Influence

The Medicis were a wealthy merchant family of Florence. They rose to fame in the 15th century after Giovanni de Medici set up a successful bank. At the time, Florence was recovering from a dreadful plague and economic disasters. Medici money revived the city. Giovanni's son Cosimo became the primary figure in Florence in 1434. For most of the next 200 years, the Medicis ruled the city-state. They even married into royalty. Both Catherine de' Medici (1519–1589) and Marie de' Medici (1573–1642) were queens of France. Four of the Medicis became Popes. They were Leo X (1475–1521), Clement VII (1478–1534), Pius IV (1499–1565) and Leo XI (1535–1605).

▲ Leading members of the Medici court, created in the workshop of Mannerist artist Agnolo Bronzino (1503–1572)

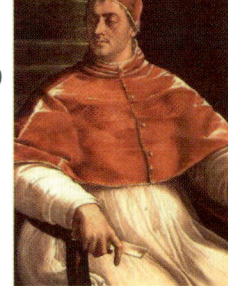 

▶ Paintings of Pope Clement VII during different stages of his life, by High Renaissance artist Sebastiano del Piombo (1485–1547)

▲ The Coronation of Marie de' Medici by the Baroque-period (17th century) genius, Peter Paul Rubens

Godfathers of the Renaissance

The Medicis were famous supporters of art and architecture. Their wealth allowed them to commission books, churches, sculptures, frescoes, paintings and all manner of valuable and beautiful objects. As a result of their interest, Florence attracted intelligent and talented men from everywhere. Among them were such talents as Brunelleschi, Masaccio, Donatello, Ghirlandaio, his pupil Michelangelo, Raphael, and many, many others. The Medicis also traded with major cities of Europe. Thus, they were able to acquire books and artworks from other parts of the world. The stability and generosity of the Medicis led to the Renaissance in Florence.

◀ Ghirlandaio's unique Confirmation of the Franciscan Rule depicts the Pope blessing St Francis. In the foreground, the Medici sons climb up the stairs with their tutor. Waiting to receive them is a dark-haired Lorenzo de' Medici, also known as Lorenzo the Magnificent

In Real Life

The Medicis not only patronised art and architecture, but also supported science. They funded the famous scientist Galileo Galilei, the father of modern astronomy. Galileo also taught the Medici family. When he first discovered the moons of Jupiter, he named them after the Medici sons. This was changed by later astronomers to honour Galileo himself.

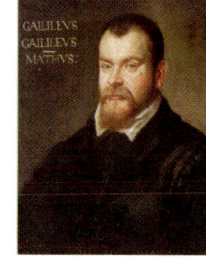

▶ Galileo Galilei, by the Venetian portrait painter Domenico Tintoretto

RENAISSANCE ART

 ## Cosimo de' Medici (1389–1464)

It was under Cosimo de' Medici, the Elder, that Renaissance Florence began to take shape. Under his orders, numerous churches were built. Among them is San Marco, whose walls bear frescoes by Fra Angelico. Cosimo also commissioned the opulent Medici Palace, built by architect Michelozzo, a follower of Brunelleschi. It was decorated with magnificent paintings. Notably, a chapel inside contains Benozzo Gozzoli's fantastic *Procession of the Magi* stretching over three walls. Cosimo not only assured the artists of sufficient work, but also treated them as friends instead of labourers. Upon his death, the people of Florence named him *Pater Patriae* (Father of the Country).

▲ The Procession of the Magi on the east wall; the golden-haired boy on the white horse represents the youngest Magi. He is drawn in the likeness of young Lorenzo de' Medici, who grew up to be Lorenzo the Magnificent. Behind him, at the head of the procession are two old men in red caps. These are Cosimo and his younger brother Piero Medici

▲ Detail of the youngest Magi

▲ Detail of Cosimo and Piero

 ## Il Magnifico (1449–1492)

Lorenzo de' Medici was the principal citizen of Florence through the peak of Florence's Renaissance. He was nicknamed Il Magnifico (The Magnificent). He was as lavish as Cosimo in acquiring great works of art. Lorenzo himself was a talented poet. Artists under his patronage included Botticelli, Perugino, Ghirlandaio, Verrocchio, and Verrocchio's pupil, Leonardo da Vinci. It was in Lorenzo's sculpture garden that a young Michelangelo learned the Classical Arts.

◀ Botticelli's Adoration of the Magi shows several members of the Medici family. Lorenzo or Giuliano stands with his sword to the far left; Cosimo is seen kneeling before the infant Christ

Pope Leo X (1475–1521)

Lorenzo's son and the first Medici pope, Leo X drew artists away from Florence to Rome and the Vatican. He borrowed and spent a lot of money to support the arts and even to fund a war. Leo X is often called the last of the High Renaissance popes. The artist Raphael greatly benefited from his efforts and created many iconic works of art.

◀ In 1518, Raphael painted a realistic portrait of Pope Leo X as a middle-aged man whose face reflects the turmoil (unrest) of his rule. He is shown with the cardinals Giulio de' Medici and Luigi de' Rossi

▲ Ceramic artist Nicola da Urbino created this large dish showing Pope Leo X presenting a baton to Federigo II Gonzaga

Italian High Renaissance

The Quattrocento unofficially ended in 1503 when Cardinal Giuliano della Rovere became Pope Julius II. The Renaissance of 16th-century Italy is called Cinquecento. Its first three decades saw the flowering of Renaissance art. This period is called High Renaissance. While the Medicis in Florence fostered Early Renaissance, the Popes paid for High Renaissance, centred in Rome. Separate schools of talent developed in Venice. The ideals of Classical and Humanistic art dominated painting and sculpture. Various techniques of perspective, shading, etc., were mastered to enhance Realism. The period began to decline after the Sack of Rome in 1527, when artists were forced to flee the city.

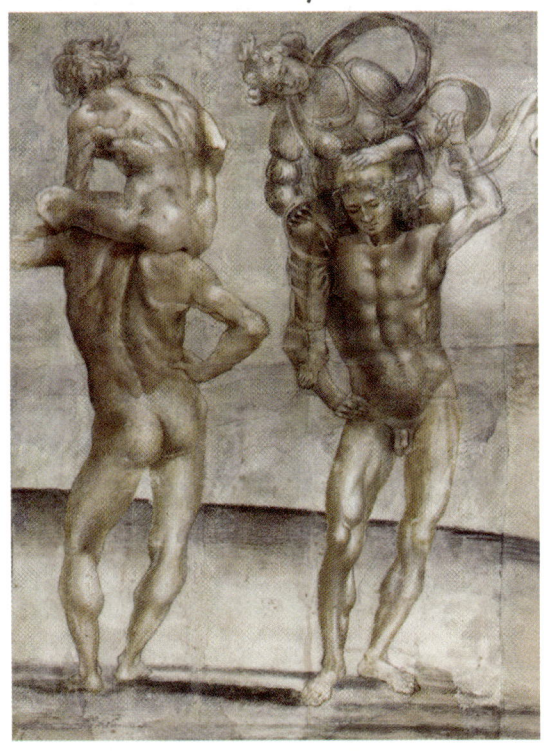

▲ Artist Luca Signorelli's sketches show his attentiveness to human detail

▶ Raphael's Mass at Bolsena depicts a 13th-century miracle. As seen in the zoomed-in panels, the artist painted himself, Pope Julius II and the Pope's daughter Felice della Rovere into the fresco

Leading Lights

High Renaissance in Rome was led by three geniuses. Leonardo da Vinci, the master of oil painting and **sfumato**; Michelangelo, the greatest sculptor and fresco artist of his time; and Raphael, the finest painter of the period. Also noteworthy were Fra Bartolommeo and Andrea del Sarto (1486–1530). Outside Rome, the extraordinary Correggio (1494–1534) was the leading painter of the Parma school. His *Assumption of the Virgin*, painted onto the dome of Parma Cathedral, contained three-dimensional illusions of heaven. The frescoes of Luca Signorelli (c.1445–1523) can be seen in the Sistine Chapel and Orvieto Cathedral. They are said to have influenced Michelangelo's own masterpieces.

▶ Fra Bartolommeo's Pietà shows dramatic depths and was inspired by the masterpieces of Michelangelo and Raphael

RENAISSANCE ART

▲ Correggio's Assumption of the Virgin (1526–1530) seems to spiral upward into the sky. It marks the path of the Virgin to Christ, who is seen waiting for her in heaven. The superb fresco had a deep impact on later artists

▶ Portrait of a Young Man, by Andrea del Sarto who was called an artist senza errori (without errors)

In Real Life

Leonardo da Vinci studied many subjects during his life including anatomy, flight, nature, mechanics and so forth. His interests were so varied, he was constantly moving from one thing to another. As a result, he had little time to paint. His fame rests on just a handful of completed masterpieces.

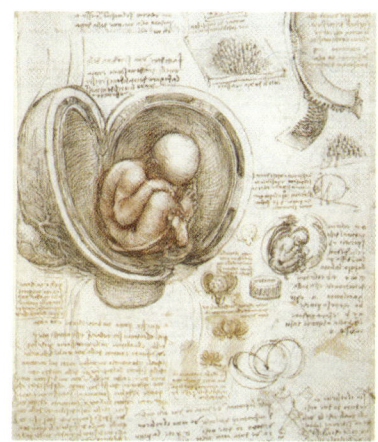

▲ A page from da Vinci's journal shows a baby growing in its mother's womb, a part of his research into human life

High Renaissance Aesthetics

Oil painting became immensely popular during the Renaissance. It allowed artists to add layers of colours, varying tones and details till perfection was achieved. Realism was still the main goal. Yet, High Renaissance art began to pay more attention to beauty and harmony. Nature was not simply copied as is. Instead, it was depicted in its most dramatic or graceful moment. Like the ancient Greeks and Romans, Renaissance artists were looking for truth in natural forms. This led them to create ideals of perfection.

▶ The Tempest, one of the earliest realistic landscapes, was the work of Giorgione, a High Renaissance talent of Venice

The Perfect Human

The idealism of High Renaissance led artists to look for the 'ideal' human—one of harmonious build with muscular grace, oval face, triangular forehead and a straight nose. Such a figure can be seen in Raphael's paintings and Michelangelo's sculptures. This manner of thinking, which attached more importance to human beings than to God, is called Humanism. It is expressed even in the religious works of High Renaissance artists. Such paintings would glorify Man, not God. However, there were still some mythological works that glorified God instead of Man. This is best seen in Correggio's *Jupiter and Io*, where the Roman god Jupiter meets his lover Io in the guise of a cloud.

▶ Jupiter and Io by Correggio

Leonardo da Vinci (1452–1519)

A true Renaissance man, Leonardo da Vinci was an inventor, artist, scientist, engineer and architect.

He kept over 13,000 pages of journals with drawings on his observations of the world. He also drew designs for inventions—hang gliders, helicopters, war machines, bridges, musical instruments, water pumps, and much more. As a master of oil painting, da Vinci perfected the techniques of *chiaroscuro*, which is a way to use shadows to create 3D effects. He was also known for *sfumato*, the use of slightly different shades of colour to move gently from light to dark. Both techniques can be seen in his most famous painting, the *Mona Lisa*.

▲ A red chalk sketch of Leonardo da Vinci, thought to be a self-portrait from c.1512

▲ The Virgin of the Rocks places its figures in a pyramidical arrangement. Unlike most religious paintings set in golden light, it is painted in a mysterious, cave-like setting which showcases Leonardo's refined chiaroscuro

▲ Study of horses, c.1490

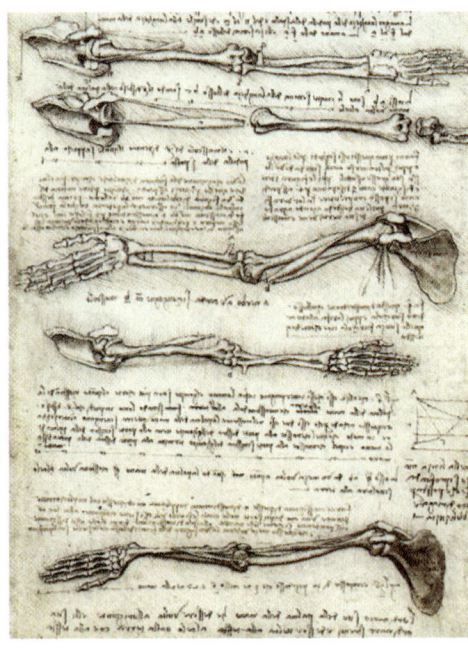

▲ Leonardo's study of an arm shows how movement changes its shape

A Perfectionist

Da Vinci strongly believed in bringing scientific observations into art. By his own count, Leonardo dissected 30 corpses in his lifetime! As a result, he had a deep understanding of muscles, bones and organs in the body. He learned to match expressions such as smiling and frowning with the movement of facial muscles. This allowed him to make amazingly realistic drawings.

Saint Jerome in the Wilderness

Around 1482, Leonardo was going through a difficult time. He painted his inner turmoil into his most melancholic piece, *St Jerome in the Wilderness*. The Christian saint fasted for years to purify his soul. Leonardo's unfinished painting shows a painfully thin man in a rocky desert. His face is twisted in suffering. His only companion is a lion, who stayed with the saint after he healed its paw.

▶ St Jerome in the Wilderness shows Leonardo's humanism and his mastery over light and shade

The Last Supper

One of da Vinci's masterpieces is a mural called *The Last Supper*. The artist began the painting around 1495. It shows Christ and his disciples at the table. In the scene, Christ announces that one of his disciples will betray him. Da Vinci's painting shows the disciples taken aback in shock and disbelief. The artist began the painting around 1495. He carefully arranged and grouped the figures to balance each other out. However, each disciple reacts in a different way. Each person's thoughts and emotions are mirrored in his body language and expressions, as perceived by da Vinci. It reads as a study of human emotion. The serene figure of Christ is in the centre.

In Real Life

The Last Supper is not a true fresco, since it was not painted onto wet plaster. Because of this, the painting began to decay quickly. Although experts have restored the mural, little of its original paint remains.

▲ *Da Vinci's The Last Supper graces the wall of the Santa Maria delle Grazie in Milan, Italy*

The Mona Lisa (c.1503–1519)

The amazing *Mona Lisa* is believed to be a portrait of Lisa Gherardini, wife of a Florentine merchant. The painting showcases Leonardo's sfumato technique. The lines are soft and blurred, not sharp and clear. This gives the portrait a much more realistic look. Notice how soft shades, and not lines, create her lips, brows, face and fingers. The strokes of paint were applied in an irregular manner to make the grain of the skin appear more lifelike. Da Vinci played with light and shadows to create depth. It created the *Mona Lisa*'s most famous feature—her mysterious smile.

▶ *The Mona Lisa (also known as La Gioconda) is shown at the Musée du Louvre in Paris*

Isn't It Amazing!

X-ray tests have shown that there are three older versions of the *Mona Lisa* under the present one! The painting was once stolen from the Louvre in Paris in 1911. However, the thief had trouble selling the painting that became famous due to the theft and it was recovered two years later.

Michelangelo (1475–1564)

Nicknamed Il Divino (the divine one), Michelangelo di Lodovico Buonarroti Simoni was a painter, sculptor, architect and engineer. He revolutionised Classical ideas about the human body. He believed that the plain, unrobed human body could express all emotions. He imbued his statues with muscle, movement and incredible power. Such a use of nude figures greatly influenced Western artists of later times.

▲ Madonna of Bruges, 1504

▲ The Crouching Boy, c. 1530–1534

▲ Doni Tondo, c. 1504–1506

Apprentice Years

Michelangelo was born to a family of declining minor nobility. During his time, noblemen did not become artists as it was considered a step down. Thus, Michelangelo **apprenticed** at the somewhat late age of 13. He joined the workshop of Florence's famous Renaissance painter, Domenico Ghirlandaio. The talented teenager soon caught the attention of Lorenzo the Magnificent. He became a part of Lorenzo's household, where he met the greatest scholars of the era.

▲ Battle of the Centaurs, 1492

▲ Bacchus, the Roman god of wine, one of Michelangelo's early sculptures, 1496–1497

Pietà

When Lorenzo de' Medici passed away, Michelangelo was only about 17 years old. Yet, he travelled to Bologna and eventually reached Rome in 1496. Here, he made his great masterpiece, the *Pietà*. The sculpture shows the Virgin Mary grieving over Christ's body. It shows the artist's deep understanding of composition. He moulded the block of stone to show various contrasts—man and woman, vertical and horizontal, dead and alive, clothed and bare.

◀ Pietà, 1498–1499

David

In 1501, Michelangelo began his next masterpiece. For Florence's cathedral, he created the gigantic marble statue *David*, using geometrical formulae from Classical times. He did not however make the statue perfectly symmetrical. This made *David* truer to life. The statue is often considered an ideal form of humanity.

Incredible Individuals

Michelangelo is the first Western artist whose biography was published while he was still alive. It was written by artist and historian, Giorgio Vasari. Unfortunately, Michelangelo did not like it. So, he had his assistant Ascanio Condivi write a new one.

◄ The statue of David, 1501–1504

Michelangelo in Rome

In 1505, Pope Julius II commissioned Michelangelo to build him a magnificent tomb. The original plan had over 40 statues. But the design had to be scaled down eventually. The marble Moses on the tomb represents an imposing and important figure in religion. Michelangelo also made two other sculptures of slaves for the tomb. But he gave these to Roberto Strozzi, who took them to France and presented them to the king.

▲ Moses for the tomb of Pope Julius II

▲ The Rebellious Slave and Dying Slave, which Michelangelo gave away

The Last Judgement

In 1534, Michelangelo made a grandiose fresco for Pope Paul III. It shows Christ the Judge surrounded by saints, apostles and martyrs. Some souls are saved, some are damned. Towards the bottom, Charon the boatman ferries souls to hell, a scene from Classical mythology.

► The Last Judgement, on the altar wall of the Sistine Chapel

The Sistine Chapel

The Apostolic Palace is the official home of the Pope in the Vatican City. Here, the Pope's chapel is named the Sistine Chapel. It was built for Pope Sixtus IV (thus, the name Sistine) by the Renaissance architect, Giovanni dei Dolci. While the building looks plain from the outside, it is richly decorated inside with frescoes and tapestries. The most breathtaking sight is the ceiling, which was painted by Michelangelo. Of these paintings, the scenes from the *Book of Genesis* are the artist's most recognisable work.

Pattern on the Walls

The paintings on the walls are arranged in three sections. The lowest portion has tapestries of gold and silver designed by Raphael, depicting events from the Gospels. The middle tier is painted in two series, the life of Moses along the southern wall and the life of Christ along the northern. The uppermost portion depicts portraits of the popes.

▲ *The tiered paintings on the walls of the Sistine Chapel*

Early Frescoes

A number of Florence's early Renaissance masters decorated the Sistine Chapel. These included Michelangelo's teacher Domenico Ghirlandaio, Botticelli, Cosimo Rosselli and Luca Signorelli. The Umbrian artists Perugino (c.1450–1523) and Pinturicchio (c.1454–1513) also added their frescoes.

▲ *Crossing of the Red Sea by Rosselli, 1481–1482*

▲ *Ceiling of the Sistine Chapel with the Genesis frescoes. The Last Judgement appears on the far wall*

RENAISSANCE ART

Ceiling Fresco

In 1508, Pope Julius II (Sixtus IV's nephew) commissioned Michelangelo to paint the **barrel-vaulted** ceiling of the Sistine Chapel. Michelangelo took four years to complete the frescoes. He painted each part of the ceiling while carefully balanced on a high platform. He used a plaster mixture called **intonaco**. This gave the paintings a brighter colour and made them more visible from the floor far below. The entire ceiling is covered with the Genesis frescoes. They are a sequence of nine images of the creation of the world, stories of Adam and Eve, and stories of Noah. The prophets and sibyls who foretold the birth of Christ are painted at the sides.

▶ *The Separation of Light from Darkness*

The Flood

Michelangelo began by painting tales of Noah over the entrance. He then moved towards the altar, painting the stories in the opposite sequence. The scene of the Great Deluge shows Noah's Ark in the background. Noah and the other survivors are safely aboard while the rest of humanity struggles frantically to find a place of safety against the rising flood.

◀ *From the Noah series, the Flood*

Michelangelo's Genius

The first figures and scenes that Michelangelo drew on the ceiling were careful, small and stable. As he painted some more, he grew more confident. He worked faster. The figures became bolder with free movements and complex expressions. All the figures show the colossal strength that is a hallmark of Michelangelo's work. The ceiling is special because it shows both the heroic and tragic tales of humanity.

▶ *In the Last Judgement fresco, Michelangelo painted St Bartholomew with his own flayed skin in hand*

▲ *Painting of a Libyan Sibyl*

Adam and Eve

Michelangelo took a year-long break while painting the ceiling, and the frescoes show this passage of time as there is a strong emotionality in the later frescoes that is missing from the earlier ones. The next work, *The Creation of Adam*, is monumental and suffused with emotion. It is Michelangelo's most famous piece. The entire scene shows a thoughtful restraint, making this one of the most expressive masterworks of the Renaissance.

▲ *The Creation of Eve* ▲ *The Creation of Adam*

Raphael (1483–1520)

Master painter and architect of the High Renaissance, Raphael is best known for his work in the Vatican. He is also famous for his many paintings of the Madonna. Though his life was short, his days were full of activity and he left behind many amazing pieces of art. He even ran a large workshop and was one of the most influential artists of Rome.

▲ Raphael's magnificent La Disputa was painted for Pope Julius II's room. It shows God, the prophets and the apostles above a gathering of the Roman Catholic Church, representing the triumph of the Church

▲ The Triumph of Galatea (1511) is Raphael's more secular and mythology-oriented work

Early Years

Raphael was born in Urbino, in Italy. His father, the painter Giovanni Santi, was his first teacher. However, Giovanni passed away when his son was only 11. Raphael then joined the workshop of the great Umbrian master Pietro Perugino. Here, he picked up a great deal of professional knowledge. He was also influenced by Perugino's quietly exquisite style. Perugino's *Christ Handing the Keys to St Peter* inspired Raphael's first major piece, *The Marriage of the Virgin* (1504).

▲ Raphael's The Marriage of the Virgin

▲ Perugino's Christ Handing the Keys to St Peter, a fresco in the Sistine Chapel

The Young Master

By 1500, the young Raphael was already a master in his own right. His expertise can be seen in an altarpiece that he helped paint in 1502. Around the same time, he painted an important piece called *Coronation of the Virgin* for the Oddi Chapel. This is the first of many paintings that tells a story. Others from a few years later include *Vision of a Knight*, *St George and the Dragon*, *Three Graces* and *St Michael*. Each piece is done with youthful freshness yet shows the artist's skill and control.

▶ The Coronation of the Virgin shows the empty tomb of Mary, who has been raised to Heaven and crowned by Christ

RENAISSANCE ART

▲ St George and the Dragon and St Michael Overwhelming the Demon show Raphael's budding interest in martial subjects

▲ Painted much later in life, this second St Michael Vanquishing Satan shows the artist's more mature work on the same subject

The Florentine Madonna

By 1504, Raphael was in Florence and learning from the works of great Renaissance artists. He was particularly influenced by Leonardo da Vinci's *sfumato*, which is the use of soft shading (instead of lines) to create forms. However, Raphael went further in creating new types of figures. Also, while Leonardo and Michelangelo painted intense and dark emotions, Raphael painted gentler expressions. The most important work of this time is a series of Madonnas. It includes the *Madonna of the Goldfinch* (c.1505), *Madonna of the Meadow* (c.1500–1505), *Esterházy Madonna* (c.1505–1507) and *La Belle Jardinière* (c.1507).

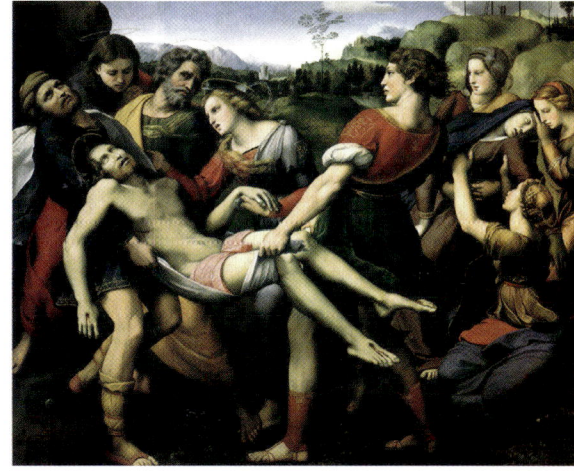

▶ In The Deposition (1507), Raphael explored the techniques of Michelangelo to depict the strength of human figures, while developing his own storytelling style

The Rome Madonna

The later Madonnas of Raphael are more energetic in movement. This can be seen in the sophisticated pose of the *Alba Madonna* (1510). The *Madonna di Foligno* (1511–1512) and the *Sistine Madonna* (1513) are richly coloured and more grandiose in composition.

◀ The Liberation of St Peter, in the Stanza d'Eliodoro room, is a night scene. It is unique for using three forms of light—a torch, the moonlight and supernatural light from an angel

⭐ Incredible Individuals

In 1508, Pope Julius II called Raphael to Rome. Raphael's personality, charm and artistic talent made him immensely popular. Giorgio Vasari dubbed him the 'Prince of Painters'.

▶ A self-portrait, around age 23

The School of Athens

Among Raphael's most famous paintings is the *School of Athens*. It shows the ancient Greek philosophers Plato and Aristotle striding forward in discussion. Famous poets, mathematicians, dramatists, philosophers and leaders of the past surround them. These are symbols of human knowledge, who represent the birth of new ideas.

Stanza della Segnatura

The *School of Athens* adorns one wall of the Stanza della Segnatura in the Vatican. The Pope worked in this room. It was originally meant to be his library. Thus, Raphael painted it with frescoes that inspire thought and reflection. On the opposite wall is the equally amazing *Disputa*, which symbolises religious faith and practice. Raphael also painted the two remaining walls. These showcase smaller frescoes called the *Parnassus* (which symbolises literature) and the *Cardinal Virtues*. Altogether, the paintings show contrasting religious and secular beliefs.

▲ The Stanza della Segnatura with the School of Athens on the wall to the right

▲ The School of Athens with Plato and Aristotle at the centre

Portraits

Raphael painted the historic figures with some well-known Renaissance faces. The tall central figure of Plato, with his flowing beard and hair, is thought to be a portrait of Leonardo da Vinci. The philosopher Heraclitus is seen sitting on his own, brooding. His figure is believed to be inspired from Michelangelo, who had a similar brooding nature. Raphael used this overlap of past and present figures on purpose. He meant to show how the Classical masters and the Renaissance greats held shared beliefs.

▲ Michelangelo as Heraclitus

▲ Identified as the mathematician Euclid, the bent figure in red robes is thought to be a portrait of the great Renaissance architect Donato Bramante

RENAISSANCE ART

Plato & Aristotle

The two main figures in the work are clearly Plato and Aristotle. They are placed under the main archway and at a distance which automatically draws your eye to them. This is a deliberate play on perspective by Raphael. The two men stand for two different schools of philosophy. The elderly Plato points a finger to the sky. He believes that the "real" world is not physical but spiritual and abstract. His student Aristotle throws his arm out towards the viewer. Aristotle believes that knowledge comes from observation and experience of the physical realm. The various other scholars are arranged on either side of Plato and Aristotle, depending on each man's beliefs.

Socrates

The brilliant Greek philosopher Socrates stands to the left of Plato. Raphael painted him using an ancient bust for reference. He is cloaked in a long robe. He holds up his hand in a gesture that is considered characteristic of the philosopher. The group that he is addressing holds his most famous students, General Alcibiades and the philosopher Aeschines. Some experts believe that the figure of Alcibiades is in fact Alexander the Great.

▲ *Socrates with his students. The womanly figure below them is thought to be Hypatia. She was a wise mathematician, philosopher and teacher of ancient Greece*

Pythagoras

The genius Greek mathematician Pythagoras is the centre of another group. He sits holding a large open book and inkpot. Looking attentively over his shoulder is Ibn Rushd, more popularly known as Averroës, the brilliant Muslim polymath and philosopher.

▶ *Pythagoras and Averroës*

In Real Life

Like many modern scientists, Pythagoras believed in both science and spirituality. Though grounded in mathematics, he believed that upon death, the immortal soul was reborn in a new body.

Renaissance in Venice

The Quattrocento was a significant period for Venice. The city was located at the crossroads between the Byzantine East and the Gothic West. It was wealthy, well connected and had a successful government headed by the Doge (dukes). After the fall of Constantinople in 1453, Venice attracted the brilliant minds of the Christian and Arabic East. It also attracted Renaissance masters from Europe. As a result, Venetian Renaissance was an amazing mix of cultural forces.

▲ Carpaccio's rich and bustling court scene is the second painting from the St Ursula series of wall paintings in Venice

▲ Renaissance portrait by Lazzaro Bastiani of Francesco Foscari, who was the Doge of Venice from 1423 till 1457

Venetian Trends

While Florence focused on composition and shading, Rome addressed dramatic movement and Venice perfected the use of colour. Perhaps, the last was inspired by the sea and by the network of canals that ran through Venice. From the time of Vittore Carpaccio (c.1460–1525), painters tried to capture the dazzling lights reflected onto the buildings and bridges. Artists drew bustling landscapes of 15th-century Venice, with its *gondolas* (rowboats), festivals and religious processions.

▲ The Miracle of the True Cross at the Bridge of San Lorenzo by Gentile Bellini

▲ In the Arrival of the Pilgrims, a 1490 painting from the Legend of St Ursula series, Carpaccio shows Attila the Hun, who has taken over the city, being informed of Ursula and the pilgrims' arrival

The Bellini Family

Venetian Renaissance was founded by Jacopo Bellini (c.1400–1470) and his sons Gentile (c.1429–1507) and Giovanni (c.1430–1516). The Bellini's huge workshop received many patrons and taught many artists. Giovanni was one of the first here to adopt the Flemish technique of oil painting. His works focus on naturalism. He united the Italian attention to anatomy with the Dutch sense of realism. His skill with oil painting techniques created incredible depth and glow while giving an almost photographic realism to his paintings.

◀ Giovanni's portrait of Doge Leonardo Loredan is realistic and forceful. The artist rejected the early Renaissance manner of painting profiles. Instead he chose a three-quarter view of the subject

▲ Gentile Bellini spent a year at the Ottoman court and painted amazing portraits like that of Sultan Mehmet II in 1480

RENAISSANCE ART

▲ Gentile's Procession of the True Cross in the Piazza San Marco shows Venice in the late 1400s

Giorgione (c.1477–1510)

Giorgione was a master at colouring. His most famous piece is *The Tempest* (see p. 15). His *Three Philosophers* is a skilful expression of light. It shows the three ages of man. The three men are thought to represent different philosophical movements: ancient thought, Arabic philosophy and the Renaissance.

▶ The Three Philosophers, 1508–1509

Titian (c.1490–1576)

A celebrity artist, Titian painted amazing landscapes with intimate groups of people. His *Noli me Tangere* shows the Garden of Gethsemane, where Mary mistakes Christ for a gardener. Against this gentle backdrop stands the risen Christ warning Mary Magdalene not to touch him, because he is soon to ascend to heaven, and he doesn't want his followers to get attached to his physical being. The figures express intense emotion.

▶ Titian's self-portrait

Tintoretto (1518–1594)

Jacopo Robusti, called Tintoretto, was the last of Venice's Renaissance masters, and also a revered Mannerist painter of the Venetian school. Tintoretto composed paintings with an eye for the effect created by light and space.

▲ Tintoretto sacrificed naturalism and used distorted forms and colours to communicate strong feelings and a supernatural eventfulness in the Last Supper

▲ In the Transportation of the Body of St Mark, Tintoretto uses a diagonal composition that pulls the viewer's eye at an angle from figure to figure

Mannerism

Mannerism arose during the later years of the Renaissance. The Italian word *maniera* means manner or style. Mannerist art is a bridge between the High Renaissance and the ornate Baroque art that followed it. It began in Florence and Rome, and then spread to the rest of Europe. It remained highly popular until artists like Annibale Carracci and Caravaggio revived Naturalism and brought Mannerism to an end.

▶ *Caravaggio paints the calling of St Mathew realistically, with stark lighting and without angels or any supernatural elements. It marks the end of Mannerism and the beginnings of Baroque*

Mannerist Painting

Mannerism came about as a reaction to the Classical and idealised styles of the Renaissance. Ignoring some of the strict Renaissance rules of harmony and proportion, Mannerism is a less natural and more exaggerated form of art. For instance, human figures are made much longer than normal and painted in artificial poses. The lighting and colours were often bold to the point of garish. Sometimes, early Mannerism pieces (c.1520–1535) were even called anti-Classical. Later, it developed into High Mannerism (c.1535–1580), which is a more intricate and meditative style. High Mannerism art was often created for sophisticated and wealthy patrons of art.

▲ *Pontormo's Deposition from the Cross shows a mass of people in a flat space. The necks and bodies are exaggerated, twisted and stretched in various poses*

▲ *Rosso Fiorentino's Deposition from the Cross shows angular figures and hurried movements, set in an almost geometric design*

Mannerist Artists

Elements of Mannerism can be seen in the later works of Michelangelo, Raphael and Correggio. Other Renaissance artists such as Rosso Fiorentino and Jacopo da Pontormo also broke away from Classicism and began indulging in Mannerist styles. They painted long limbs, small heads, stylised expressions and agitated emotions. Followers of Raphael, like Giulio Romano and Polidoro da Caravaggio, also emerged as Mannerist artists.

◀ *Giulio Romano's Fall of the Giants creates the illusion of a dome. In the centre, Jupiter sends grotesque giants crashing down with thunderbolts for daring to invade Mt Olympus*

RENAISSANCE ART

🏛 The Sack of Rome

On 6 May 1527, armies of the Holy Roman Emperor Charles V stormed through Rome, looting and killing everything in sight. This brought an end to the Renaissance movement in the city. Artists of the new Mannerist movement fled for their lives. They took the style to other parts of Italy and Europe. Among them were Francesco Salviati, Domenico Beccafumi, Federico Zuccari and Pellegrino Tibaldi. The most important of them was Bronzino, who became the greatest Mannerist painter in Florence at the time. The Dutch cities of Haarlem and Amsterdam welcomed the new style. In Prague, Emperor Rudolf II became its most ambitious patron.

▲ *Fire Sent Down from Heaven by Beccafumi (1538–1539) at the Pisa Cathedral*

▲ *Haarlem-based Hendrik Goltzius was one of the most technically skilled Mannerists. See his sophisticated use of lighting and detail in Sine Cerere et Baccho friget Venus (Without Ceres and Bacchus, Venus would freeze)*

🏛 Parmigianino (1503–1540)

The Italian artist Girolamo Francesco Maria Mazzola is better known as Parmigianino. He was one of the earliest and most influential Mannerist artists. Parmigianino himself was deeply influenced by Correggio. This can be seen in his first important piece, the *Mystic Marriage of St Catherine* (c.1521). His Mannerist art was characterised by icy lighting, distorted spaces and unnaturally long forms. All these elements give his works a strange emotional intensity. After the sack of Rome, Parmigianino left for Bologna and then Parma, where he created masterpieces like the *Madonna with the Long Neck*.

▶ *Madonna with the Long Neck (c.1534) shows the elongated features that are a hallmark of Mannerism*

🏛 Sculpture

The sculptors Bartolomeo Ammannati and Benvenuto Cellini made extraordinary Mannerist sculptures. However, perhaps the most complex and graceful statues come from the Mannerist master Giambologna.

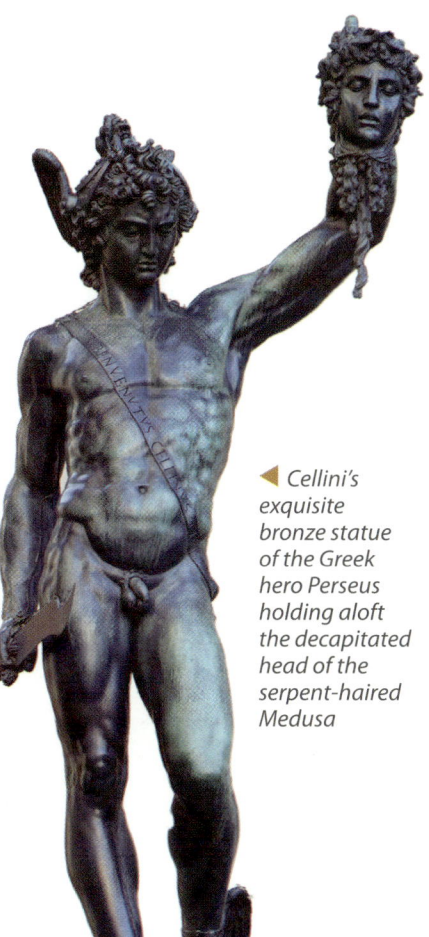
◀ *Cellini's exquisite bronze statue of the Greek hero Perseus holding aloft the decapitated head of the serpent-haired Medusa*

◀ *Florence's famous Fountain of Neptune, designed by Bartolomeo Ammannati*

El Greco (1541–1614)

The Greek-born Doménikos Theotokópoulos was a master of Spanish painting during the Mannerist period. His paintings were so far ahead of his time, they left many of his contemporaries puzzled. It was only in the 20th century that his art came to be really understood. He also worked as a sculptor and architect. While he was living in Italy, he was given the name by which he became famous, El Greco (the Greek). He never forgot his Greek origins and always signed his work using his full and original name.

◀ *The Agony in the Garden of Gethsemane, c.1590, shows Christ and an angel against a foreboding background. The apostles are asleep in a cocoon, while in the distance Judas approaches with soldiers*

◀ *The Vision of St John (1608–1614) shows how markedly different El Greco's art was from Renaissance art. It is said to have inspired the 20th-century genius Picasso to paint Les Demoiselles d'Avignon (The Young Ladies of Avignon)*

Expressionism

El Greco's highly individual and dramatic style makes him neither a Renaissance painter nor a true Mannerist. Indeed, his work is closer to the Expressionism style of much later centuries. El Greco is best known for his religious paintings. These show long, tortured-looking figures on unnaturally coloured backdrops. The paintings are a mix of eastern (Byzantine-Greek) and western styles. The intensely spiritual result was very attractive to the Catholic Church of Spain. Thus, El Greco was welcomed with open arms to the country.

El Greco's paintings are often tumultuous, with a rhythm like the broken waves of a sea. Light seems to emanate from within the characters that adds drama to the art.

▲ *The Adoration of the Name of Jesus is a great example of the themes El Greco usually explored*

▲ *El Greco's art was unlike anything ever seen in or before the Mannerist period. His Baptism of Christ is one such example*

RENAISSANCE ART

Rejecting the Renaissance

In the 1560s, El Greco went to study art in Venice. He joined the studio of Titian, who was then the greatest painter in Italy. El Greco naturally studied the works of the Renaissance masters, particularly those of Michelangelo, Raphael and Titian. Yet, he refused to submit to their artistic beliefs. He believed in his own talent and was determined to create his own form of art. This was easier to do away from Italy. Thus, in 1577, he moved to Toledo, Spain.

▶ *The Penitent Magdalene*, one of the first works painted in Toledo, shows Titian's influence on El Greco

Spain and Fame

El Greco made a name for himself when he did a set of paintings for the church of Santo Domingo el Antiguo in Toledo. He then created two pieces for Philip II of Spain, the *Allegory of the Holy League* and *Martyrdom of St Maurice*, in 1580–1582. Unfortunately, the king did not like the latter painting, and El Greco was no longer associated with the Spanish court. In 1586, he painted the amazing *Burial of the Count de Orgaz* which soon became his most famous work. Over time, El Greco's paintings became less descriptive and more dramatic. He drew the human body taller and paler.

El Greco's Painting

The almost violent way in which El Greco painted his pieces shows an early form of Expressionism. They are far from the Realism and Naturalism that were popular with artists and patrons of his time. Most important in his work is his use of light. Many of his figures seem to be lit from within. Sometimes, they reflect a light from some unknown source. The flashes of light give way to swirls of gloomily clad figures, half-hidden threats and distorted gestures. Each painting is a thrilling puzzle of emotions.

▲ *Burial of the Count of Orgaz*, 1586

◀ *The Assumption of the Virgin*, one of the paintings at Santo Domingo el Antiguo that made El Greco famous

▲ *The View of Toledo* is one of two surviving landscapes of the city painted by El Greco

Isn't It Amazing!

El Greco said of Michelangelo that he was a "good man, but he did not know how to paint." Despite this, Michelangelo has a strong influence on some of El Greco's works, such as *The Holy Trinity*.

Word Check

Anatomy: It is the structure of a living being, including the relative position and function of all parts.

Annunciation: It is the moment when the archangel Gabriel tells Mary that she will become the mother of Christ.

Apprentice: This refers to a person who acquires skills from a master for a period of time for low wages.

Baptistery: It is the part of the church where the ritual of baptism is held.

Barrel-vaulted: It describes a ceiling that is curved in a half cylinder like a barrel.

Bust: It is a sculpture of the upper part of a human being, from head to chest.

Condottiere: It is a soldier who could be hired for money, which was a common practice in 15th-century Europe.

Draughtsman: It is a person who draws accurately with technical mastery.

Humanism: It is the belief that the needs and values of human beings supersede religious dogma.

Intonaco: It is an Italian word for the thin layer of plaster on which an artist paints a fresco. The painting is created while the plaster is wet so that the pigment penetrates into it.

Patron: It refers to a person who supports an artist or writer by paying for their works and supporting their livelihood.

Polyptych: It is an artwork that is made up of a number of attached panels.

Renaissance: It refers to the period between the 14th and 16th centuries, when there was a revival of European scholarship and art under the influence of Classical models.

Sfumato: It is a form in painting where there are no clear lines. Instead, form is created by shading or blending colours.

Surreal: It means that something seems fantastic or unbelievable in a dream-like manner.

Symbolism: It is a method of using symbols to represent an idea or quality. Symbolism also refers to an artistic movement where people used symbolic images or ideas to convey their emotions, mystical ideas or state of mind.

Three-dimensional: It refers to objects that have length, breadth and height. It is also simply called 3D. Paintings can be thought of as two-dimensional (2D), because they have no real height. Thus, artists use various tricks and techniques of perspective to show us real-life 3D objects on 2D paper.

Tromp l'oeil: It is the style of painting that creates the illusion of three dimensions.